LEADERSHIP

CRISIS

MANAGEMENT

UNDERSTANDING THE

3-STAGES

OF CRISIS MANAGEMENT

MARK VILLAREAL

ISBN: 978-1-7323085-6-5

Copyright © 2020 by Mark Villareal

TABLE OF CONTENTS

FOREWORD

A crisis can happen, whether created by us or not. A crisis occurs at the least opportune time and surprises our daily routine and execution as an organization. Just when we believe we can relax, everything is going well, and all is well, a crisis can and will occur and turn our confidence into a panic. Those of us that believe we are prepared will be tested and a crisis brings out and defines true leadership. It is easy to be a leader when everything is going right, and we may have earned the benefit of a well-established team that executes. But what we do when a crisis happens can define how we lead, how our leadership team executes, and how all employees follow.

Also, what happens to an organization that is not prepared? Many organizations are ill-prepared for a crisis. They run day by day in survival mode with a lack of leadership or they are in a stage that improvements are needed in staff, and execution. These organizations believe they have time to make the necessary changes. They understand their lack of execution but believe that confronting the situation and making the necessary steps in execution does not have to happen today. Then, a crisis happens. They make erratic decisions, make constant changes, and find it hard to obtain confidence from the leadership team and employee staff. Many of these organizations falter quickly, and go out of business. Some, surprisingly, make it through. But if they do, what must they change to ensure they are not in this position again? This is what is defined in *Leadership Crisis Management: The 3-Stages of Crisis Management*.

LEADERSHIP CRISIS MANAGEMENT

STAGE #1 - PRE-CRISIS

STAGE #1 - PRE-CRISIS

Sure, now that we are all in a crisis everyone is speaking of crisis management. However, true crisis management does not start when the crisis starts. Businesses that find that they did not take necessary steps to prepare their staff, and especially their leaders for a crisis, any crisis, are the ones that will struggle more to make it through or may have already given up.

There are three basic stages of crisis management. The first stage is before the crisis ever happens. To me, this can be the most important part of the implementation and follow-through that provides success when a crisis occurs. The second stage is when the crisis hits and how you work through it. An equally important aspect of how you, as the leader, your leadership team, and your staff responds. This is when you realize what is automatic that has been created within them based upon the culture you created, maintained, and hopefully protected and executed daily. The final stage is post-crisis, which we all hope we make it to. Here we reassess, evaluate, and move forward with our action plans and execution.

Stage #1 – Foundation before the crisis.

In our Leadership Workshops, and especially in our one, two and three-day Crisis Management Workshops we teach, and yes preach about the importance of culture, what we define as good, strong, and positive culture. I have a firm belief that culture is everything. Culture defines your organization, it's the foundation, and it should define your employees from top to bottom. So when we speak of culture we start with the values and principles of your organization. The question is are they just words and statements, or do they resonate with what your organization desires and on what your employees should exhibit daily when on the job? Solid organizations list their values prominently on their website for their customers, potential customers, and all employees to see. Expedia, like other organizations, creates principle statements or what they label as their Guiding Principles and list them prominently. This tells all customers or potential customers what Expedia holds themselves accountable to, and what customers should hold Expedia accountable for. It then tells every employee, or employee candidate what your organization has committed to, and your organization should have a process that hires employees who match and commit to your values and principles. Too many organizations do not hire accordingly and then find a culture clash and they have to deal with the situation when it happens. Hiring is not always perfect, but having a process helps in communicating to everyone that your organization's culture is important and will be defended and protected. It starts in the hiring process.

Values and principles are the foundation of your organization and should guide every decision, new hire, strategic plans, and strategic initiatives. Built upon your values and principles are your Mission Statement and your Vision Statement. Based upon how you build them your Mission Statement is usually external and Vision is internal. Once again, is your Mission Statement just words or are they the vein of your very existence. Your Mission Statement needs to define why you exist, and what is your purpose? It should not be complicated but very straight forward. Your Mission Statement should be prominent on your website as a commitment to your customers and potential customers, but also demonstrates to your employees your commitments. Every employee should know and understand your Mission Statement and how it affects their role, but more importantly what it means to each customer. Being able to explain how it benefits any customer, which may vary, is the key to understanding a Mission Statement. I get surprised when I deliver leadership training on how many leaders in attendance from the organization do not know their organization's Mission Statement.

A Vision Statement is usually internal with an outlook of 3 to 5 years that defines a Big Hairy Audacious Goal otherwise known as a BHAG. This is why it is internal as it is a vision to your employees on what your organization is striving for. That BHAG is a challenge for what you are reaching for and it should be a stretch and a reach. Great leaders speak of the vision and point to milestone achievements that enlighten each employee that progress is being made and that the BHAG can be achieved. Yes, these three things, Values & Principles, Mission Statement, and Vision Statement are just the start of Stage 1 of crisis management as they are the foundation of the culture you need to create.

Why is culture so important to crisis management?

Culture is important because a strongly established culture becomes a habit and builds instincts that become automatic when problems occur and decisions need to be made. The biggest trait I always taught and coached when running teams and organizations is self-accountability. This started from the interview process and continued each day of employment. I would repeat myself constantly that the best thing any employee could do is make themselves indispensable to their employer. This is why I would teach and preach self-accountability. Certainly this is important to leaders, but we also drive it down to each employee. I would communicate from day one that my high expectations and recommendations are that each employee takes self-accountability in their personal and professional development. We established and incorporated a system and a document that provided them a way to create three goals each month. Goal #1: What one thing will they do for personal development? Goal #2: What one thing will they do for professional development? Goal #3: What one goal, with a measurement, will they achieve? I would suggest this be done monthly and that they choose a peer as an accountability partner where they meet with a peer once per month to present, discuss, and hold each other accountable. This monthly meeting takes approximately 10-minutes.

Make yourself indispensable to your employer!

I wonder how many recent individuals who were recently downsized wish they had made themselves indispensable? How does one do this? I would educate from day one my recommendation that each employee embraces our values and principles, drive our mission and vision, and inquire how they could advance each and align their development around them. I would suggest and recommend that each employee understand the organization's strategic initiatives, and once again ask how they can contribute to their achievement. I suggested they ask how they can align their skills and knowledge in development to enhance their contribution to achieving the organization's initiatives. Imagine having to downsize, which unfortunately happens, and having to decide between an employee who embraced and executed in these areas, and one who just maintained the status quo. Great cultures teach and allow employees to embrace and take self-accountability in their development. Also, it eliminates the culture of entitlement from day one, and I would simply communicate that when promotions or times of investment for one's development arises that those that take and demonstrate self-accountability would help make my choice easier.

Make everyone a problem-solver!

This is something we teach in our leadership courses that if you empower your staff and teach them to become good problem-solvers then your job becomes easier. One would think this would be obvious to teach your leadership team, yet many organizations lack in the execution of teaching and empowering leadership staff to problem-solve. Then when a crisis occurs panic happens, instead of the instinct and action of problem-solving skills that have become natural due to leadership staff being empowered and trained. In our workshops we teach a problem-solving process that starts with defining the problem and working the process through to a solution. Great leaders teach and encourage their leadership staff to solve problems and make a decision. When a member of the staff makes a decision they should be complimented for the decision, and then coached by walking through their thought process. I would explain, that if my decision may have been different, I would coach why the difference. Each time I had a coaching engagement with a staff member on decision-making, they grew and developed more. Jack Welch of GE fame once stated that the worst decision is a non-decision. I remember once taking over a business that needed a turn-around that my Operations Manager would bring to me what they deemed a problem and wanted to show we could not do certain things to solve it. However each time they would bring a problem we would walk through the process and we would come to a solution. After a while this person started to bring the problems with possible solutions scenarios as they were learning from the process. Then they finally stopped bringing me problems because they were solving them already. In fact, in that one business location that was a turn-around situation, we had four of our managers over a short period, recruited by the corporate office of a 260 location franchise organization, to be Regional Managers for the worldwide organization. Our team was filled with problem-solving leaders and problem-solving, self-accountable employees. In three short years that one location was sold for approximately 12-million dollars.

Teach the 7-Habits of Highly Effective People.

Learn from the masters. Habits are everything and they create instinct. The 7 Habits of Highly Effective People instills instinct in everyone who learns them. The habits are, be proactive, begin with the end in mind, put first things first, think win/win, seek first to understand and then be understood, synergize, and finally, to sharpen the saw. Embracing the 7-Habits puts everyone on the same page of a thinking process, and it works in all areas, sales, leadership, life, and everywhere else. The 7 Habits teaches any leader and employee staff to pause, and walk through the habits. The power of thinking about beginning with the end in mind, or seeking first to understand helps eliminates rash decisions. Everyone understanding the 7 Habits creates an understanding of the vocabulary when used in daily actions. The best habit you can demonstrate as a leader is to be visible, transparent, over-communicate, and to confront issues and not hide. This will be important when a crisis occurs. The best character test and habit you can instill in your team is the statement that bad news does not get better with time. It is not always easy, but bad news will always be addressed.

Teach a First Team Environment.

This is from The Five Dysfunctions of a Team. Dysfunctional teams lack trust and therefore are afraid of being vulnerable. A dysfunctional team tolerates and allows gossip, resentment, and the lack of owning decisions. A First Team Environment teaches that gossip is not tolerated, and others will push any resentment or disagreements towards a first-team conversation. A first-team environment teaches that opinions and feedback are welcomed professionally. Strong disagreements are allowed, properly, and in the right fashion, as this helps in creating and working towards the best decisions. However, once leadership makes the decision, everyone owns the decision. Remember, that a true leader is not a builder of consensus but a molder of consensus. Everyone had their input, but whether their input was adopted does not factor in the commitment that they will own the decision as a member of the leadership staff. When a crisis occurs, gossip, rumors must not be allowed, and the best way is to create that environment is to already have it instilled in the existing environment.

Earn respect, as a leader that is genuine and authentic.

As a leader, it is imperative and valuable to be looked at as being genuine and authentic. Also, respect is earned daily and built stronger over time. When I would take over a team or businesses I would make it a point to show up early and stay late to have simple conversations to learn about my employees and have them learn about me. This is where they built their belief system on my authenticity and genuineness. Respect was earned by my actions, and most importantly by my consistency. As a leader I worried more about being respected than being liked. You will find that being consistent, genuine, and authentic that your team will appreciate those traits. What this creates is the belief and understanding that although you may as a leader be faced with difficult decisions, your staff of all employees will know and trust that you will make each decision with everyone's best interest in mind. Your ultimate responsibility is the health of the organization. Crisis, when they occur, will bring difficult decisions and having this instilled already in the culture makes the transition minimal.

Always be coaching, assessing and evaluating.

Part of leadership is to assess our people, which is our leadership team, and staff. I believe all leaders need to understand that being a leader is being a coach. The great coach Mike Krzyzewski of NCAA Basketball fame, once stated that "I think of myself as a leader who happens to coach basketball." His emphasis is that he is leading. However when you lead you must assess your staff, evaluate and consistently provide feedback. You create and execute development plans to identify your staff members' strengths and weaknesses, and how to improve in each area. You create and look for coaching opportunities so you gain perspective on each person's growth, behavior, and potential. Leaders create processes so they know the capabilities of their team in action, that when a crisis occurs they can rely on that development. They are cognizant of the strengths, weaknesses, and knowledge of each team member, and have built up a solid team of internal trusted advisors.

Build a network of mentors.

One thing my mother would teach me is to always look for mentors to help me grow and develop. She would also encourage me to mentor others as I would learn and develop from the process. CEO's join CEO groups that work well for them that has other CEO's of other industries where they learn from their organization, and they mentor each other. I recommend that all leaders look to build relationships with trusted mentors, and this is something done over time. Mentors do not have to be in the same industry as your organization, and those outside your field of expertise add value. When a crisis occurs, mentors will provide value to seek feedback and gain an outside perspective. The lack of building a support network of mentors becomes more apparent when a crisis happens and trusted outside feedback would add value, yet it is not available.

Be a servant leader that focuses on the success of others.

I am a firm believer in servant leadership that focuses on the success of others, which drives the success and the culture of the organization. Servant leadership builds a culture that infects and affects everyone, it is contagious in a good way. A leadership team that is built on servant leadership still must execute difficult decisions, but over some time has earned the trust of the employees. A servant leadership led team takes the hard decisions at face value, mourns for a moment, and then focuses on what it takes to pull the organization through to success. Finally, there is much more on culture-building that enhances Stage #1, but it is this stage that is where most organizations lack. Then when these skills, knowledge, and leadership traits are needed from the leadership team and employee staff, it is not there. Chaos and panic occur. This does not mean that every organization that does this will survive, but it will give them a fighting chance over others in their industry. When a crisis occurs, instinct takes over and not paralysis. Solution mindsets come into action, and not random decisions. As the leader, you have a staff of trusted advisors who have developed a first-team environment where opinions, disagreements, and feedback is welcomed, structured and respected. Your decision-making process is taught, is automatic, and executed by instinct.

LEADERSHIP CRISIS MANAGEMENT

STAGE #2 - THE CRISIS HAS LANDED

STAGE #2 - THE CRISIS HAS LANDED

"During a crisis things fall fast under bad leadership."
John Maxwell

This is a great quote by John Maxwell that emphasizes the point that an organization may survive under bad leadership, and many do. But an organization under bad leadership when hit with a crisis, the fall is faster. Things that were being held together, day by day, fall apart. Dissatisfied employees that would bite their tongue and keep their opposing opinions silent, will speak out, gossip, and create division among the team. The silent naysayers who quietly would question the decisions of leadership will proudly proclaim, "I told you so." This is why stage #1 is so important, but unfortunately the weakest point of most organizations. The old statement that perception is reality truly becomes your reality.

Remembering your foundation of values, principles, mission and vision.

One of the first items to portray is remembering the values and principles your organization adopted, employed, and built your culture around. A firm foundation is built for when times are difficult to make it through the trying times. The first thing a leader must do is recognize the event and situation, gather the leadership team, and remind them of the foundation that they built. The leader should do this with all staff as well, so all leaders participate and witness, and then support the message moving forward. The first thought process and priority is an assessment of the facts and consequences of what has transpired. Some events may be uncertain, to begin with, and the first thought and hope are that things can hold together for the short term. But it is the responsibility of leadership to keep assessing and finding facts.

Leaders take responsibility, accountability, and give credit.

I once read from a leadership consultant that a leader takes the blame and gives the credit. The true message is a leader takes the responsibility, accountability, and gives the credit. The difference is sometimes the cause of a crisis is not created by the organization, such as the recent virus known as COVID 19. But when the situation happens the leader and leadership team moves forward with execution. The leader, from that point, takes responsibility, assumes accountability, and gives the credit. Each leader needs to take responsibility, accountability, and give the credit as well for areas they are responsible for. Their natural instincts, built within their skills and knowledge of the problem-solving need to take over and should be automatic. This is from the culture that was built in stage #1, their instincts developed from the daily process and executing problem-solving. Note why stage #1 is so important. This is also why a preset formula on teaching problem-solving skills is built around a sound set of a system and process of gaining understanding and resolution. With my teams, our system of problem-solving was built around a baseball diamond, and it also what we teach in leadership workshops today. We start at home plate and we label home plate 'values and principles.' One reason we chose to teach on a baseball field is with the concept that where you start, home plate, also is where you want to finish by going around the bases and scoring. The true message that if we start with values and principles, which is our foundation, we will want to finish with values and principles as we define and execute our process of problem-solving. It places the emphasis on the high value of your values and principles. Whatever the solution, you want your values and principles maintained.

First base was reserved for whatever hindrance you as an individual have as a leader. For example, some leaders make decisions in anger, so this must be addressed before moving forward. Other leaders race to make decisions and take a shortcut in the process, which can blind the individual to important information. This can cause several situations. The first is when a shortcut goes astray, you have to backtrack to where you started the shortcut. Causing a loss of time. The second scenario is having perceived success with the shortcut which creates the habit of taking more shortcuts. When a leader develops the habit of taking shortcuts, they are missing important data that could have a profound effect on their long-term results. Next is second base, where you define exactly what the problem is. We teach a standard set of questions in our workshops that help break down needed information in determining exactly what the problem is. Your leadership team must have a process taught from the top down that all members are familiar with, and have confidence in utilizing. Third base is where we teach defining a solution, by putting forth what is known. What can be assumed by an educated assumption, and what are the best choices, pros and cons, and what would be the best plans. John Maxwell likes to state, what is Plan A, and what is Plan B? We then create a plan and execute it. Your plan needs to be systematic, and all educated on the process.

Place your top advisors and experts around you, and seek additional experts if necessary.

As mentioned in Stage #1, as the leader, you developed a process that you have assessed your team, understand each member's strengths and weaknesses, and have prepared them to be problem-solvers. When a crisis occurs the first thing that must be executed is an initial assessment of the crisis. A crisis comes in many forms. Many are just specific to your business. Loss of financial backing, quick and high turnover of key personnel and other factors are a few that can happen. There is some crisis that is created that can be industry-specific, such as new regulations or compliance rules, to crisis that causes issues for all businesses, such as one that affects financial markets, which then affects the revenue flow of your business. When this occurs, it is recommended that you meet with your first team of advisors, which is usually your first level of leadership that you have developed to be problem solvers. If a crisis is determined to be industry-specific then having an industry expert, or resource for information available will be important. This is also why in Stage #1 you have built a network of mentors and those you mentor. Great leaders welcome and seek experts when needed. This is executed easier with an already pre-built support network.

There are several questions to define, with the first being what is the crisis? How did it develop? Is it temporary, which is defined as 30-days or less? If internal to your business is there anything that is pressing and that needs to be done to eliminate loss, pain, or damage? The same can be asked if it is more external, industry-specific, or of catastrophic potential. Catastrophic are those that create quick financial stress, which can be by industry or by other outside factors. Recognizing what the crisis is, and acknowledging that there is a crisis or potential crisis to the business, is an important aspect of leadership.

Choose, plan, do.

This step is following and implementing your problem-solving process. Getting your team members involved who should already understand the process, and be comfortable in offering opinions and feedback without being fearful of being vulnerable. Because of implementing and establishing the first-team environment, your team is ready for the execution of working through problem-solving of the crisis. Remember Step #1 of problem-solving is to start with your values and principles. Because where you start is where you want to finish. Every decision you make needs to be measured against your values and principles, and your mission. Re-emphasizing these at the start allows you to work the 7 Habits and incorporate them through the entire process. When you are within crisis management, it may be difficult to see where you can be proactive. But in the execution plan you build, you must ask within the plan where can you build in proactive steps? Next, you need to list out, 'Start With The End In Mind' and ask constantly with the team what is the end in mind as you define the problem, and each underlining circumstance created. This should help guide your decisions. The next habit of 'Putting First Things First' is what the team needs to be challenged with. What are the first items to put first? What are the most pressing issues? Certainly, anything that is causing harm, then anything that has the potential to create and cause harm should be at the top of the list. Then, to think win/win is a good mindset, and in a crisis may be challenging and have a degree of difficulty. Finally, to 'seek first to understand, then be understood' is an important factor. What needs to be clarified more, or maybe misunderstood? Here is where you may also implement educated assumptions on possible scenarios and their consequences. Note there is a difference between educated assumptions versus blind assumptions. Finally, synergizing is what you are doing as a team, and because of an effective Stage #1 implementation and execution, your team is used to working through this process naturally. Now, you can see as a leader, why working and creating a First Team Environment, developing as a team the 7 Habits of Highly Effective People, and educating all leadership and staff as problem solvers, that you have built an effective resource for addressing the crisis.

Create a plan, with accountability and responsibility.

Now that your team has broken down the problems, scenarios, and worked the 7 Habits to flush through what is the end in mind. It is now that you must build a plan, make decisions, and assign tasks, responsibilities, and specific accountability that allows everyone to be on the same page. With all plans you must build in a defined evaluation process that allows you to assess and measure progress and success. In crisis management, this may be with more frequency than normal planning, as adjustments and focus must be quick and decisive. Here is where you will utilize your standard process for business planning, that your business has established. I personally utilize the process taught in the Rockefeller Habits. This teaches planning and focuses daily, weekly, and includes a Manager Accountability Plan the breaks down each task, responsibility, accountability, and timeline. This helps in ensuring that everything is tied to a SMART Goal, which means that they are specific, measurable, achievable, relevant, and time-bound. Business plans need to be thought of as a roadmap, or what now would be called a GPS with today's technology. Any roadmap has a starting point, and an endpoint. But they also have a time table, with milestones in between. This is important as the milestones will allow leadership to understand, and communicate that progress is being made, as the staff needs to believe there is a light at the end of a tunnel. However, and much like a true roadmap, it will demonstrate that if you strayed from the roadmap due to a roadblock, where you need to get back on track. As the leader you need to gain insight, and then be a molder of consensus for what is best for the business as a whole. What is best for the business as a whole should also be what is best for the employees. But it must be thought of with the focus on the business, as a healthy and financially responsible company is best for the business as a whole, and for the employees. However if downsizing is part of the business plan, this is why the focus on the business takes priority because ultimately it is being responsible to those you keep, and hopefully those you may bring back as you make it through and survive and start to rebuild and flourish.

The business plan or Manager Accountability Plan must be broken down with each task, and who owns the task, and who has a specific responsibility to execute with a timeline on every item. Each team member must understand the plan, whether they have a specific task or responsibility or not. They need to have a comprehensive understanding as they will be counted on for assessment, feedback, and peer to peer support and accountability. They need to own the decisions, the plan, its execution, and its results as if they built every item themselves. They need to support, and show support, and rally the troops as part of the leadership team. When you hit inflection points, or evaluating points within the timeline, the whole team, or members of the team need to participate in the evaluation providing direct and honest feedback. You are in a crisis, and there is no time to waste for lack of confronting issues. Here is the time that leaders need to either lead, follow, or get out of the way. If some items need adjustment, redirection, or Plan B, then make the decision, communicate, and execute. The most important factor is building as solid as a plan from the beginning, hopefully eliminating too many wholesale changes that occur from poor planning. Here is where you can lose support and create a belief that you might not succeed.

Some of my best mentors and CEO's have advised, that if you have to downsize personnel, to try to take the mindset to cut as deep as you can, that prevents you from having to come back and cut some more later. The second round of cuts can cause concern and once again create a belief that you might not succeed. Remember, that although you built a First Team Environment, a time of crisis might bring out an individual or two, who are naysayers. The inflection points for naysayers increase if you have to make more cuts, and alter the direction of your Management Accountability Plan too often. We always state in leadership training, that if you believe that you are not being watched as a leader, you are fooling yourself. During a time of crisis, leadership being watched is amplified, and you want to portray and earn confidence.

Communication, transparency, and visibility.

The best thing any leader can do is to communicate with all staff, not just the leadership team. The staff needs to be confident during uncertain times. Great leaders should always communicate often, share the vision, thank their people, and point to victories. This is even more important during times of crisis. Employees, customers and vendors need to have the trust that leadership is available, is willing to communicate, and not in hiding. Years ago in a turnaround situation, when leading an organization that was in debt and working to overcome the adversity in the daily operations. I accepted every phone call whether from a customer, or from a vendor, for complaints. With customers I had a customer service process that we teach in our workshops for addressing complaints and concerns but ultimately earning the trust from the customer that we were correcting any and all issues. With vendors, I was aware that prior management would avoid their calls and have them sent to voicemail. It was important, that I would take all calls, pleasant or not. Unfortunately with vendors, I could not always inform the vendor what they wanted to hear, that I would pay them that day. But I did communicate the plan I had, and that I will always be available and not avoid them. Within 3-years we sold that business unit for 12-million dollars. At that time I had asked some of the vendors why they stayed with us. Their common reply was that we had the integrity to not avoid them. We would communicate, and we earned their respect. This will be much the same with your employees.

Optimism, vision, and insight.

When communicating, a leader needs to explain the facts. They need to define that a plan has been developed, and explain an outlook on that plan that communicates confidence. You need to remind the employee staff, that even if they are not in management, that they can display leadership. Here is a good moment to ask and encourage leadership from everyone.

During a crisis, a leader needs to display optimism to all employees and point to milestone achievement and small victories. As stated, it is leadership that displays and exhibits that there is a light at the end of the tunnel. A leader needs to communicate the vision, whether it is for the day, week, month, or year. Great leaders communicate the vision constantly. A leader needs to provide insight, gain insight, and at times, seek insight. In addition, a leader needs to be cognizant of naysayers, and maintain a strong culture. Finally, they need to evaluate and assess the leadership staff and employees on their development and daily execution during the crisis. The leader needs to coach constantly and continue to help their people develop. Many future leaders develop and showcase their abilities during a crisis.

LEADERSHIP CRISIS MANAGEMENT

STAGE #3 - POST CRISIS

STAGE #3 - POST CRISIS

Stage #3 is post-crisis, and we certainly hope your organization made it through. Be thankful if the organization did survive, and be grateful to your leadership team, and employee staff. Reach out and show appreciation to your customers, and with your vendors. Relationships and partnerships should be strengthened when having gone through a crisis.

The assessment and evaluation.

"Wow, now everything can go back to normal!"

Many of us may have this thought. Is the thought real, and should it be? Think about it. You have made it through a crisis, either short, long, or somewhere in between. Certainly, and at times we may take pride in a given situation, which is okay. However I always remember what my mom once taught me, "Your ego is not your amigo." In other words don't let ego create a roadblock and let everything just go back to the way it was before the crisis. You owe it to your organization to take a step back, and assess how you and the team managed through the crisis, and evaluate what changes, if any, you need to execute.

Knowing you will evaluate after the crisis, as the leader you should keep a journal throughout the process and the execution. Note changes that were made after initial planning. Also note each individual's contribution and effectiveness, and the growth of individual staff members. Be factual and honest about disappointments, whether in performance, execution, attitudes, reactions and overall culture. You need to evaluate if the 7 Habits, Business Planning, First Team Environment, and other important aspects like peer to peer accountability held together. We recommend that you do a self-assessment on yourself, and an assessment from your perception on the leadership team, and employee staff members. Executing a leadership 360 is also recommended. This is where others on the leadership team assess you, and can also assess other peers. You can even expand a 360 where employees assess staff. The main premise is understanding what was learned from the crisis? What can be gained, and what is missing that needs to be learned?

Stage #1 assessment and evaluation.

When I work with organizations through crisis management, the biggest part of the assessment and evaluation is understanding how the organization was prepared. Truly what is being asked here is when the crisis happened was it evident that the organization had a strong stage #1 process and that the team was as ready as possible. A crisis can still shock individuals and cause legitimate concerns. But the assessment on how the team performed and an evaluation of the skills, knowledge and traits in action as a leader through the crisis is important. If you believe your organization executes stage #1 consistently, and effectively, then it should have been evident when the crisis occurred. Certainly this does not mean that you did not have to coach, as that should have been automatic and often. Coaches remind, encourage, builds confidence, push when necessary, and leads by example during any crisis. As the leader, and then also with your leadership team, define if all the stage #1 execution you believe your team executed was effective or not. In many areas that you noted that it lacked, notate the situation and define a plan to improve it. I have seen some organizations realize they did not have an effective stage #1 implementation and made it through the crisis based on luck and grit. This is when they must decide that a stage #1 program must be implemented. If that is the determination, then build an action plan with a timeline and execute it. Note all action plans must have SMART Goals, accountability and responsibilities noted.

Most organizations determine that they were somewhere in between when assessing and evaluating how effective and evident stage #1 preparation and execution was when the crisis happened. They find areas that through the assessment they did well. Then in specific areas they may find that they did not execute well, and it became evident during the crisis. Here is also where the items must be notated, and an action plan built around improving in this area, and then set into action.

Assess and evaluate staff.

The assessment and evaluation of staff are important for several reasons. How leadership staff performed is a telling sign of additional knowledge, skills, and traits that need to be developed and enhanced. Each of these should be noted and we highly recommend that development plans are created for each staff member coming out of a crisis. The plans should be simple, yet specific, and must have two-way buy-in. Two-way buy-in is where the individual assessed themselves too and both parties meet to build a simple two-page plan.

But here is a key question? Are there any leaders from the leadership team that did not perform to standards that they are a concern moving forward? Sometimes this is the hard part of business, and this person may have given effort but just did not have the ability. Remember, your best interest is for the whole organization and coming out of a crisis your mandate is to do everything for the health of your organization. This is both financially, and with the quality of the staff. Assess, and make the difficult decisions that are necessary and decide any changes and adjustments quickly.

The next portion of the staff is the employee ranks, and as mentioned, they do not have to be managers to be leaders. Assess, or have your leadership team assess who stepped forward and made good impressions. Who demonstrated that they have the attributes of a future leader? If any, and build a plan that keeps them developing. For the other employees, provide additional training as a reward for them pushing the organization through the crisis. Finally, were any employees a concern, that behavior modification had little or no effect, that you need to make a decision?

Assess and evaluate the competition.

Finally, based upon what the crisis specifics were. If it affected your industry and other organizations downsized or closed down, how is the state of your competition now? Are there key, quality personnel available that your organization can benefit from? Great sports teams are always looking to upgrade their team, and great teams fight to stay competitive each year. Make the choices that adhere to your commitment to strengthening your organization.

The question I always ask an organization is, what gives you a strategic advantage in your industry? When I ask this, many have no answer. We recommend you define this for your organization, and after a crisis determine if it is still the same, or does it need to change. Sometimes it may be strengthened and other times it may be weakened. Many times after a crisis when evaluating competition an organization can define and realize a new strategic advantage and build a plan around it. When this is done they put a new focus on the strategic advantage and walk it through the process identical to building strategic initiatives. This is executed this way so all areas of the business know where they play a role and an action plan is built and executed. Marketing may change or be enhanced, as well as sales and operations. When coming out of a crisis it is imperative that you come out demonstrating purpose, confidence, and leading your team fighting.

Commit your organization to success.

If you survived a crisis as an organization and you do not demonstrate to your employees a plan of confidence moving forward, then your culture will slide backward. Whether your culture was solid before the crisis, or whether it was mediocre or poor, you must now understand that you need to lead, follow, or get out of the way. I hope you lead. By leading you must demonstrate resolve, resilience, determination, and confidence by building and communicating your vision moving forward. You must educate on milestones, goals and objectives, and you must point to small wins. You must demonstrate authenticity, transparency, and confidence in your plan. You need to demonstrate, that with whatever changes and adjustments you made, that you did so with the organization's best interest in mind.

ABOUT THE AUTHOR

Mark Villareal is a Three Time International Best Selling Author.

His Mission Statement is: "To elevate leadership one person, one team and one organization at a time." His passion is to make an impact daily through public speaking, coaching and consulting.

He believes that great leaders pay it forward, and having been blessed with a 35-year career in the business world, building businesses, mentoring and aspiring leaders, and making a difference in people's lives both personally and professionally has been the ultimate reward. He believes, coaches and teaches servant leadership that defines and builds the culture in organizations that creates long term sustainable results.

Visit Mark at: www.markvillareal.com.

Printed in Great Britain
by Amazon